Beauty and the Broken

7 STORIES OF PEOPLE LIKE YOU AND ME

BEACON HILL PRESS

OF KANSAS CITY

Beauty and the Broken

7 STORIES OF PEOPLE LIKE YOU AND ME

Editor
Mike L. Wonch
Director of Editorial
Bonnie Perry
Writer
Jennifer George

Copyright © 2015 by Beacon Hill Press of Kansas City

Beacon Hill Press of Kansas City
PO Box 419527
Kansas City, MO 64141
nph.com

ISBN: 978-0-8341-3430-0
Printed in U.S.A.

10 9 8 7 6 5 4 3 2 1

CONTENTS

There are times in life when we go through circumstances that lead us to think, "Why is this happening to me?" Often, during dark times, we may have feelings of loneliness, despair, and anger. In the midst of these situations, we may think we are alone. While no two people can go through the same situation in the same way, we can learn from those who have traveled the same path.

Beauty and the Broken shares true-to-life stories about people like you and me. These stories invite you to identify with the characters and think about the ways they faced the difficulties of life. Each narrative also leads you to think about your own life and how, with the power and presence of God, you can overcome anything life throws your way.

The purpose of this book is not to give you advice on how you should think, feel, or act. However, the hope is that as you enter the life of each character, you will begin to think about your own life and the ways in which God can be your source of guidance, power, and strength. As you read each narrative, prayerfully ask God, "What do You want to teach me through this story?"

Jennifer George is a former WordAction curriculum editor. She lives with her husband and two children in rural Arkansas. Her novella, Bufflye, *appears in* Youth Imagination, *a Silver Pen literary magazine.*

Forgiveness/ Reconciliation

And when you stand praying, if you hold anything against anyone, forgive them, so that your Father in heaven may forgive you your sins.
Mark 11:25

A loud wail woke Dottie from shallow sleep. Startled, she threw back the covers and tried to swing her legs over the side of the bed, reaching for her glasses at the same time. Only her legs didn't move. A sharp pain reminded her that she had broken her hip two weeks earlier. She winced and gasped.

The poor, young-sounding girl on the other side of the privacy curtain cried and moaned so loudly, and for so long, the nurse quickly came in to give her something so she would rest. Dottie lay quietly, hearing the conversation behind the thin screen.

"Please, princess," a man said as soon as the nurse left. "She's been waiting out in the hallway all night."

"She can sit there forever. I don't care. She's a murderer," the young girl said, sobbing.

Dottie heard a women's voice say quietly, "Now Kayla, I don't think Madeleine tried to murder anyone. She wasn't watching the road."

"What difference does it make? Deonte is dead because of her!" Then, Dottie heard the young girl (Kayla) sobbing very loudly as the women simpered and shushed her.

Unable to sleep, Dottie turned on her light and tried to focus on reading the devotional book her pastor, her only visitor this week, had brought her. More than once, she whispered the prayer, "Lord, let me be an instrument of Your peace here." She couldn't help hearing what was going on behind the curtain throughout that night, and she began to piece together that Kayla and her boyfriend were riding home with Madeleine from a church youth group outing. They were speeding, and as they tried to pass a semi on the wrong side, the car crashed into a guard rail, killing Deonte. Kayla had spent some time in intensive care because of an internal injury, but Madeleine was only bruised and not otherwise hurt. Kayla had missed Deonte's funeral, and grief overtook her whenever she remembered this.

Through the opening in the curtain beyond the foot of her bed, Dottie could see the shelf on Kayla's side of the room loaded with flowers and balloons. Dottie looked at her own empty shelf and sighed. She would have loved for someone to miss her and send her flowers. She shook her head to push away the thought. What was done was done, and she needed to move forward instead of pining away for the past. But every time Kayla growled, "I hate her," and "I'm never going to forgive her for this," Dottie cringed.

One evening, the curtain was left open, and the unfortunate roommates saw each other for the first time. Kayla had a cast on one leg and the opposite arm. She had a bandage covering part of her forehead and her shoulder on the same side.

"I believe we're both a mess," Dottie said, motioning to the black boot cast on one leg and the large, bandaged wound on the other. "Thank goodness they don't let us out at night here. We'd never come back in one piece."

Kayla laughed and said, "It's too bad. I was going to say we should go sledding tonight."

Dottie laughed. "Maybe next week," she said.

Thus began their unlikely friendship. Kayla gave Dottie a crash course in being eighteen. She introduced her to all kinds of ridiculous television shows and songs, which Dottie was surprised to find she actually enjoyed. Kayla's friends came by every day and kept her laughing. They also gave Dottie candy and soda from the stash they had brought for Kayla.

One morning, Kayla's cell phone rang, and she growled, muttering, "Ignore."

"Madeleine again?" asked Dottie.

"I hate her!" She rolled her eyes and huffed a sigh. Her youthful beauty nearly disappeared with her tight scowl and narrowed eyes.

"But wasn't she your best friend?"

"Was. As in past tense."

Dottie wrinkled her brows in concern, but didn't push any further.

After Kayla's father had gone home for the night and her mother was asleep on the guest couch, Dottie asked, "Kayla, are you a Christian?"

"Yeah," Kayla answered, looking up from her phone, its screen casting a bluish glow on her face. "Why? Are you?"

"Oh, yes," she said. "Can I ask you another question?"

"Sure," Kayla answered. She put down her phone and looked at Dottie expectantly.

"You're pretty angry with your friend Madeleine, aren't you?"

"Angry doesn't cover it. I hate her."

"So you've said. Has she asked you to forgive her?"

"Sure. But she killed someone. Someone I happen to love. It's not like she borrowed my favorite shoes and ruined them. This is so much bigger than that. This is unforgivable." The girl's voice broke.

"Is it? I know your heart is broken. But what if you refusing to forgive Madeleine binds up God's blessing in both of your lives?"

"What?" Kayla's voice had a sharp edge.

Dottie closed her eyes and recited, "Truly I tell you, whatever you bind on earth will be bound in heaven, and whatever you loose on earth will be loosed in heaven."[1]

Kayla rolled her eyes. "I've gone to Sunday school my whole life, Dottie. I don't think that verse is talking about car accidents."

"Are you sure? I think just a few verses later it says we must forgive those who sin against us seventy-seven times.[2] We're not meant to stay angry. If you refuse to forgive her, not only do you prevent God from doing good things in your life, but you are forcing that poor girl to carry around guilt that she doesn't want to hold onto anymore."

Kayla's brows came together and her lips pursed. Dottie opened her mouth to say more, but she closed it again and waited. Kayla suddenly found a piece of fuzz on her blanket very interesting and began picking at it.

When Kayla didn't respond, Dottie said, "I'm not trying to make your mind up for you, but don't you think you ought to forgive your friend?"

"I don't know," she said.

"Okay." Dottie looked out the window at the street lights against the night sky. "Lord, open her eyes and help her see," she whispered.

Later on that night in the near darkness, Kayla asked, "Dottie, are you awake?"

"Sure am." It was a fact that nobody slept in hospitals, not with all the noise and interruptions.

---

1. Matthew 18:18
2. Matthew 18:21

"Well, it's my turn to ask you something," Kayla said. "We've been here forever. Why haven't you had any visitors?"

Dottie pressed her lips together before she spoke. "I don't have anyone anymore."

"No kids?"

"Well, I do have a daughter, but she doesn't come around."

"Why?"

Dottie sighed. "We had a fight years ago."

"About what?"

"I don't know. The usual stuff between parents and their children." The truth was her only child, a daughter named Carol, had left the state for a job despite Dottie's protests. Carol had left her mother behind two years after her father passed away, and Dottie resented it.

"Hm," Kayla said. "If it's not right to stay mad at someone, shouldn't you forgive her?"

Dottie's mouth quivered for a moment, but she swallowed and forced her emotions down. She joked weakly, "Who would say something like that?"

"Just a wise person I'm glad I can call my friend," Kayla said.

The next day, Kayla was released from the hospital. The bandages on her forehead and shoulder were smaller, and she was able to move enough to be helped into a wheelchair. Dottie teared up a little. She was going to miss Kayla and her goofy friends. The silence of loneliness and hurt feelings could be so deafening sometimes.

Kayla had been sitting in the wheelchair, chatting with Dottie when her mother peeked her head into the room.

"Kayla, someone is here to see you."

Kayla turned her chair around using her good foot as a petite girl with dark hair ran across the room and fell to her knees in front of her.

"Maddie," Kayla whispered, bursting into tears. She wrapped her arm awkwardly around Madeleine, pressing her forehead to her friend's. They stayed like that for some time. "I am so sorry," Madeleine wailed.

"I know. I forgive you."

Dottie couldn't understand the rest of what they were saying, but she guessed it didn't matter. Grace was happening. Dottie silently thanked God for the noisy, but beautiful, reunion.

After the girls had left, Dottie remained still. What had happened here was from God, and she didn't want to ruin the moment. Finally, she picked up the phone from the bedside table and called her pastor. "Reverend? Can you do me a favor? Yes. I'd like you to go to my house and get my address book. It's in the desk drawer in the living room. I'd like to call my daughter."

Reflect on this...

Kayla needed to forgive her friend, and Dottie needed to forgive her daughter. Who do you think would be easier to forgive? Why?

What holds people back from forgiving one another?

Just like Kayla seemed like a different person when she talked about Madeleine, we are changed when we hold grudges. Think about a situation where you noticed a person was completely, negatively changed because of a grudge.

Read Matthew 18:21–35. Secular culture tells us that betrayal calls for revenge. How does God call His people to respond when they have been wronged?

2

Repentance/
Confession

*Whoever conceals their sins does not
prosper, but the one who confesses
and renounces them finds mercy.*
Proverb 28:13

Jake flopped down on the hotel bed with a heavy sigh. He didn't want to be there. He didn't want to be anywhere. In fact, he wanted to be as far away from--well, himself, as he could get. He reached for his phone, but then he thought twice and pulled his hand back.

"You're going to have to tell Emily," Pastor Marcus' words echoed in his mind. Yes, he was going to have to tell her. But not yet. How could he? What could he say? He thought confessions were supposed to make a person feel better. Jake had not been expecting Pastor Marcus to throw responsibility back into his lap. He had asked God to forgive him and was determined, with God's help, to walk the path of faith. But his pastor was not willing to let it go at that.

"Your relationship with Emily has been badly damaged, even if she doesn't know it yet," Pastor Marcus had said. "If you want peace again--peace in your marriage, peace in your home, peace in your heart, then you need to make things right. It is good that you have repented. But--"

Jake had interrupted, "What if she doesn't forgive me?"

"I can't predict how Emily will react," Pastor Marcus had said. "But we can pray for God to bring about forgiveness. May I pray with you?"

Jake had let Pastor Marcus pray over the phone, but he was not really listening. He was worrying about what Emily would say. The hurt, betrayed look on her face would just kill him. He could not let her down. Not like this.

But he already had.

Jake's heart pounded hard, and his tongue felt thick and dry as he picked up his phone. He speed dialed his wife's number.

"Hello?" Emily said. In the background, there was a clatter and a screech followed by muffled whining. "Hello?" she repeated.

Jake swallowed hard and spoke. "Em?"

"Jake! Hey! Where are you?"

"I'm... um... I'm back. In town."

"Well where are you in town? I could've picked you up at the airport, but you never called." She sounded a little grumpy, which she had plenty of reason to be. Jake was supposed to have gotten home in the morning, and it was now after seven o'clock in the evening. Sophie was a handful, and Emily had all she could handle between caring for her and working her own part-time job at the bakery. When he was traveling for his sales job, the only break his wife got was when the baby was sleeping or when her own mother had time to babysit.

"I can't, Em. I can't tell you."

"What? Don't be ridiculous. Of course you can tell me. Are you in some kind of trouble?"

"No. Well, yes. Not really. I don't know."

Emily's voice switched from cross to concerned. "What's going on? Are you okay?"

"No. I'm not okay. And I can't come home." Jake sniffed hard and held back a sob.

"Why? What happened?"

"I've really messed up. Big time."

"And...you can't come home?"

"No. I got a hotel room. I need some time. To think."

"Jake--" Emily began, but Jake hung up, and turning his phone off, threw it across the room, where it landed on the floor with a muted thud. He curled up into a fetal position on the bed and lay there until he fell asleep.

Two hours later, there was a knock on the hotel room door. Jake woke up and rubbed his eyes, momentarily unsure of where he was. He glanced around, and seeing his phone on the floor by the desk, his heart sank. The knock came again.

"The sign says, 'Do not disturb,'" he grumbled.

"I know," Emily said through the door.

A jolt of adrenaline surged through him. He wanted nothing more than to run away, as far away as he could run and as fast as he could go, but he had nowhere else to go. He went to the door and fumbled with the lock as he opened it.

There stood Emily, her hair in a messy ponytail that was wet from rain. Her sneakers were soaked, as well as her jeans halfway up to her knees. She didn't smile when she saw him. She didn't berate him for not coming home or ask him any questions. She didn't say anything at all. She just stood there shivering in her oversized jacket.

"Um, hi," he said, not sure what else to say. He wanted to spill out his soul to her, to grovel at her feet and beg for forgiveness, but he couldn't even get his feet to move enough to let her through the doorway.

Emily stepped forward, gently pushing the door open herself.

"How did you find me?" Jake asked.

"It wasn't hard. There are only two hotels in town."

"Oh. Right. Where's Sophie?"

"With Mom."

"Oh."

"Jake, what is this about? Did you get fired? What could you possibly have messed up so badly that you can't come home?"

"No. No, it's not that." Jake sat down on the bed. Emily grabbed a chair and pulled it around to face him before sitting down. He leaned forward and rested his forehead on his fists. She reached for his chin to tip it up, but he pulled away.

Emily took a couple of deep breaths and asked, "Is-is there someone else, then?"

Stumbling over his words between sobs, he began to try to explain what had happened. He had reconnected with an old high school friend online, and they had begun to talk for long periods of time on the computer and eventually on the phone. They had bumped into each other at a trade show on this most recent trip. When the hotel security guards began locking up the main hall, the woman had invited him to join her for something to eat. After that..... When Jake finally ran out of words, he sat staring at the dull floral pattern of the carpet.

Emily, who had been weeping silently into her hands, whispered, "I'm not surprised."

"You knew?" Jake was incredulous.

"Well, I wondered if you would. Eventually."

"How did you--"

"You don't log off the computer before you go to bed," she said. She wiped at the smeared eye makeup with a crumpled tissue she had taken from her pocket.

"Emily, I never meant to do this to you....I love you," Jake said in a trembling voice.

He waited for her to say something more, but she didn't. After several minutes, he said, "I don't expect you to be able to forgive me. I wouldn't forgive me. I can't forgive myself. Not for this. I've hurt you. I'll stay here until I figure things out. I can get a place in town, and--"

She whispered, "This is the worst thing you could ever do to me."

"I know, and I am truly sorry" he replied.

Emily nodded and sniffled. She stood up, zipped up her jacket, and pulled her keys out of her pocket. Jake jumped up to open the door for her, but she did not follow Jake to the door. Instead, she picked up his jacket and phone and handed them to him. He gave her a puzzled look.

"Come on. Get your bag. Let's go home."

"But--"

She sniffled and said, "Get your bag. I love you for better or for worse. I didn't marry you just to end it when things got bad. I want us to work this out. I don't know if we'll ever be the same again. But I want to try." She took a step, then stopped again. "Unless you don't want to?"

"I want to," Jake whispered. He grabbed the handle of his suitcase and followed his wife out of the hotel and into the rain.

Reflect on this...

If you were Emily, what would your initial reaction to Jake's confession be?

Is it always necessary to confess to the person you have hurt or wronged? Are there ever circumstances or situations where confessing to another could do more harm than good to that relationship?

Read Jesus' parable of the prodigal son in Luke 15:11-24. Like the father in this parable, Emily goes out to find Jake and shows grace as she takes the first steps toward forgiving him and rebuilding their relationship. Think about at time when God in His grace met you where you were.

Have you ever needed forgiveness but felt you didn't deserve it? If you have found peace in that situation, how did you do it? Is there someone you need to forgive? How might the relationship change if you forgive this person?

NOTES:

3

Sanctification

But just as he who called you is holy, so be holy in all you do; for it is written: "Be holy, because I am holy."
1 Peter 3:15–16

With a groan, Melanie got out of bed. She didn't want to, but the alarm said 4:45 AM. As she got her gym bag ready, scolding herself for not doing it the night before, all the dark thoughts she'd been thinking lately went through her head again, "Why bother? You're never going to get fit and healthy. Stay home and sleep. It won't matter if you skip the gym today, or even every day. You're not making any progress."

Melanie had made progress for sure--at first. The initial New Year's resolution of "getting fit" had been difficult, but successful. She had lost sixty pounds and was on the path to getting healthy, In fact, she had stopped diabetes before it got any worse than "borderline." That was a big deal. She had just begun to not feel out of place among all the fit people at the gym-- why was she going at 5 AM., again? "Come on, Mel," she thought. "Just go. No excuses."

She pulled her blonde hair up into a ponytail, grabbed her keys and bag, and went out to the car. After starting it and putting it into gear, she threw it into park and went back into her house, opening the door as quietly as possible so she didn't wake her two kids. She found the water bottle she had forgotten on the kitchen counter, pausing for a moment at the box of donuts. She thought, "What would it hurt to have just one?" She took out a chocolate iced donut out of the box and put it to her lips for a moment. With another sigh, she put the donut back, letting herself at least lick the sticky icing off her fingers before she pulled a banana off its bunch and left. She knew that one donut would lead to a second, and a third. She was losing weight and starting to feel healthy, but there was more progress to be made.

And while she had reversed her borderline diabetes, her doctor had reminded her that she was still at a high risk for heart disease, and her cholesterol numbers painted a pretty grim picture of the future. She didn't want to die of a heart attack at age 47 like her father had. Forty-seven was only 14 years away. Her kids would not even be out of high school then.

Melanie knew why it was so hard to go to the gym. She hadn't lost an ounce in almost two months, and her cholesterol was still high enough that she might have to go on medication for it. The doctor tried to reassure her that hitting a plateau like this was normal, and that she would see success if she didn't give up. Even so, she felt like giving up.

And it wasn't just her plan to get healthy that was stalled. It was everything in her life. So many things felt out of balance, even pointless. Everything from long days of chasing after her increasingly willful kids to her part-time cosmetic business. Even church was no longer as satisfying as it had been. She prayed and read her Bible at home, but she often wondered if there was something more, something she was overlooking.

"Mel!" a chipper voice called as soon as she had put her water bottle down next to a stationary bike. It was her friend Jolene. Cheerful Jolene. Kind Jolene. Life-is-wonderful Jolene. Melanie wasn't feeling so chipper; she could have done without running into her today. Melanie really liked Jolene and often went out for coffee with her; but honestly, she just wanted to sit by herself and pout this morning.

"How are you?" Jolene chirped.

"Oh, I'm here," Melanie answered with a smile and a shrug. "That's good, right?"

"You showed up. The battle's won," Jolene said. She got on a bike right next to Melanie's.

"I guess so."

Melanie started up her bike, but she couldn't get comfortable. She tried shifting in the seat. She leaned forward and pedaled for a while with her forearms on the handles. Then she leaned back. She tried adjusting the seat height, but that didn't help either. Finally, she stopped and took a few long sips of water.

"Not feeling it today?" Jolene asked. She put her magazine down in the rack on the front of her bike.

Melanie shook her head and swallowed. "Mm-mm."

"Wanna run?"

"Me? I don't run."

"Why not?"

"I don't know. I just haven't."

"Wanna try it?"

"But I'm slow."

"That's okay. You gotta start somewhere."

Melanie had a feeling Jolene wasn't going to leave her alone to brood. "Okay. I'll try it, I guess."

Jolene smiled. "I want to show you something."

Melanie followed Jolene back into the locker room, where she pulled out her phone. She started scrolling through pictures, apologizing for taking so long. Finally, she found the one she wanted and turned the phone around for Melanie to see. In the picture was a much younger but less healthy Jolene.

"That was me at 25," Jolene said. "So I know how hard it is to start something new. But I pressed on, even when it got hard. Especially then. I'm so glad I did. Should we run now?"

That was how Melanie found herself shuffling along at barely a jogger's pace on the carpeted track around the top level of the gym. This was not the most comfortable thing in the world. She felt a little silly, but Jolene jogged alongside her, matching her slow pace. After two laps, Melanie slowed to a walk.

"I'm sorry. I just can't. Not right now," she panted.

"No problem," Jolene said. She ran a couple of laps at her normal speed, then dropped to a walk, too. "Good job!"

"I don't get how you do it. You just keep going and going."

"Forgetting what is behind and straining toward what is ahead, I press on toward the goal,"[3] Jolene said.

"That is definitely not what the Bible was talking about, Jolene."

"I know it's not, but it's still true. I have to let go of all the doubt and fear and failure and just keep trying. It's the same thing with faith. You can't let yourself stagnate."

"That's pretty much where I am right now."

"Stagnated?"

Melanie nodded. "I just feel like there's something I'm missing. Something more. And I'm just not getting it."

"Are we talking faith or health?"

3. Philippians 3:14

"Both."

"Well, we are meant to grow in our faith. Salvation isn't meant to be used only as a ticket to heaven; it's the beginning of a faith journey with God. A relationship with God is meant to change us completely. You know, make us into holy people."

"Hm," Melanie said in a skeptic tone.

"It's like this. Say the whole Christian life is a race."

"Gee, where have we heard this before?"

"Well, it is a good way to look at it. Anyway, say you sign up for the race and even show up on race day, but when the starting gun goes off, you just stand there. That wouldn't make sense, would it?"

Melanie shook her head.

"So, you have to move to get to the goal. Of course the goal is eternal life with God. But God wants to have a life-transforming relationship with us. He wants to give us the power and strength to run the race, but that requires actually running."

"So what do I do, then? To run?"

"Well, you can't do it by yourself. You have to ask God to take you deeper and deeper into your relationship with Him. He doesn't want you to show up for the race and then do nothing. He wants you to run, to give your entire life to Him, allowing Him to change you."

"Just like that?" Melanie had stopped now, and Jolene stopped next to her, wiping her face and neck with a towel.

"Pretty much, though it sounds easier than it actually is. It takes commitment, and means surrendering all to God. It means allowing God's Spirit to invade every part your life. It's all about relying on the Holy Spirit for guidance, power, and strength. It requires letting go of the reins and letting God transform your heart and life."

"Is it easier or harder than giving up sweets?" Melanie asked with a smile.

Jolene laughed, "I don't know, but you know that nothing is impossible for God. It's like running. You take that first step, and then the next, and you don't worry about 50 steps from now. You just focus on the step you're taking. You take that first step and surrender your will to God—allowing Him to take full control. He'll show you what He wants to change. Hey, I have to go now. I have to wake Kelsie up for school. See you later?"

"Yeah, sure."

"One step at a time," Jolene called over her shoulder as she headed down the stairs.

Melanie leaned against the wall to stretch her calves for a moment. After one more sip of water, she took a few slow, clumsy steps and began to jog again.

Reflect on this...

Have you ever felt like Melanie when it comes to your Christian walk?

Read 1 Peter 1:13-16. What does it mean to be holy as God is holy?

The word "holy" means set apart for God, pure, or dedicated to His service. How does that differ from the way the secular world uses the word? How easy or difficult is it for a person to be made holy?

Read John 14:15-31. In what ways does the Holy Spirit work in the lives of the believer? How does the Holy Spirit enable us to live holy lives?

Read Philippians 3:13-14. What keeps people from completely surrendering their lives to God?

4

Suffering/Sorrow/Pain

*Cast all your anxiety on him
because he cares for you.
1 Peter 5:7*

Suffering

I tried to pretend to be asleep when my dad walked into my hospital room. I found myself doing that a lot lately.

"Mail's here," Dad said, plopping a small bundle of brightly-colored envelopes on the bed right next to my face. He went over to the window and yanked the heavy maroon curtains open. I squinted against the unwelcome flood of sunlight and turned my head away. The oxygen tube got stuck between my shoulder and the bed and ripped out of my nose.

"Ugh," was all I said.

"Come on, Connor. They're just trying to cheer you up."

I coughed and stuck the tube back in my nose. "Great."

"Look, son. I know this cancer is a game changer for you."

"You mean game over."

"Don't say that! You're going to fight this."

I sighed and picked up the first envelope. On the outside of the card was printed the Bible verse, "'My grace is sufficient for you, for my power is made perfect in weakness.' 2 Corinthians 12:9."

"Ugh," was all I said. This had to be the tenth card I'd received with this verse on it. What did that even mean? People were always quoting the Bible at me these days instead of talking to me.

Dad picked up the card and read the Scripture verse aloud. "There's truth to that, son."

"Nothing is sufficient for me now. Except a miracle cure." I made quote marks in the air with my fingers.

"It's not like you to give up hope when things get tough," he answered.

"I didn't finish the marathon," I said. Instead of running across the finish line at my first marathon in triumph, I passed out at mile ten and had to be rushed to the hospital. The chest X-rays the doctors took showed cancer.

"If it wasn't for the respiratory distress, we wouldn't have caught the cancer so early."

"You have to put a positive spin on everything, don't you?"

Dad sat down on the edge of my bed and looked out the window a while before turning to me.

"Do you think—" Dad stopped, sucking in his cheeks to hide his quivering lip. "Do you really think God would willingly give any of His children a disease as horrible as cancer?"

I shrugged.

"God doesn't promise that we will never be sick. But He does promise He will be with us."

"I can't feel God with me," I whispered.

When the sun went down and he had gone home, I didn't bother turning on a light. I just thought. I hadn't thought about God in a long time, not since the first surgery had failed to take away all the tumors. I whispered into the darkness, "God…"

Sorrow

"I've never felt so lonely." Anna fiddled with the silverware on the hot metal table outside the burger stand, shivering as a sudden wind blew across her.

"Sweetie, I'm so sorry." Rosie put her hand on her cousin's arm.

"What am I going to do?" Anna sobbed, unable to quiet herself, no matter how she tried.

"Did he say where he was going?"

"No. For all I know, he's still next door."

Anna's husband, Tony, had left her after only three years of marriage, claiming he had made a mistake and never should have gotten married in the first place. He had run off with the woman who lived next door—Anna's friend—and deserted her.

"It just isn't right," Rosie said, still patting Anna's arm.

"You got that right. And what gets me the most is how he pretended to love God all this time. He faked being a Christian, just like he faked loving me."

"Oh, honey—" Rosie began.

"Whatever," Anna interrupted. "He cheated on me, and I hope he gets what he deserves."

"I don't know. I wouldn't wish that on anyone."

"Now you're starting to sound like the people at church." Anna chuckled ironically, and wiping at her eyes, nodded to the server, who was wandering around with two drinks in his hands.

"Believe me, I would take away your sorrow if I could. You're closer than a sister to me, and I love you. The people at church mean well, even if they sound like they are saying the same thing over and over."

Anna wrinkled her nose and said in a high-pitched tone, "Don't worry, Anna. God has something better planned for you."

Anna shook her head and rolled her eyes. "I tell you what, if God cares about me, then why did He let this happen to me?"

"It's Tony who chose to break your heart," Rosie answered after a long sip of soda. "God lets everyone make their own choices because He loves them, even if they break His heart."

Anna shrugged and turned her attention to her phone, scrolling through her text messages for a moment. Scrolling far enough back, she saw texts from Tony. One-word responses to questions like, "Want me to pick up dinner on the way home?" Anna's eyes filled up with fresh tears.

Rosie gently took away Anna's phone and set it on the table. The server brought out the food, and Anna suddenly realized she was hungry.

After several minutes, and half of a bacon cheeseburger, Rosie said, "Look. This divorce stuff is messy, and horrible and painful."

Anna raised her eyebrows and nodded, her mouth too full to speak.

"But I'm here with you, and I'll stick with you through all the bad stuff. I'm not abandoning you. And I assure you—it may not feel like it right now, but God isn't going to abandon you, either. He says promises to never leave us or forsake us."[4]

"Thanks."

"I know it doesn't make you feel better right now."

"No. It doesn't. It's okay." Anna took another bite of her cheeseburger.

---

4. Hebrews 13:5

Pain

Charlie went in to the office half an hour early every day so he could spend a few quiet moments with God. Some days he believed that God's strength was all that got him through eight hours in this high-stress brokerage office.

This day was no exception; Charlie sat in his cubicle with his coffee and Bible. The unusual part was the fact that his boss, Sean, showed up at the same time, a full two hours earlier than usual. A former peer of his, Sean was on the fast track to leadership. They used to joke around together at lunch, but now Charlie was filling Sean's coffee cups and making his copies. Not that it mattered— Charlie was glad just to go into work, put in his forty hours, and go home. There was more to life than work.

"Hennesy," Sean spoke suddenly behind Charlie, startling him enough to make him bumble with his coffee cup. "Put that thing away. What do you think this is a church?"

Charlie quietly slid his Bible into his desk drawer.

After giving Charlie a list of things to do, Sean said, "And I need you to get me fifteen hundred dollars from petty cash."

"Fifteen hundred?" Charlie asked. Requests were usually under a few hundred dollars.

"I don't have my debit card with me, and I need some things." Sean said.

Charlie took a petty cash request form from his desk. "Okay. I have to put down a reason for the withdrawal."

"No, you don't. No one would need to know. I'll pay it back tomorrow morning when I get paid."

Charlie fidgeted in his seat. "That's stealing."

"Whatever, Pope Charles." Sean turned and strutted away, scoffing.

Later that afternoon, Charlie found himself nervously fiddling with a pen as he sat next to Sean in the office of the company Vice President, Jack.

"You were the first one in the office today. Is that right?"

"Yes," Charlie said.

"This morning, fifteen hundred dollars was taken from the petty cash fund," Jack began. "Sean tells me you asked him to advance you fifteen hundred for rent."

Charlie nearly jumped from his seat, his pulse raising. "That's not true!"

"Are you calling Sean a liar?" Jack asked, with an eyebrow raised.

Slumping back into his seat, he sighed and said, "I guess I am. If you don't believe me, why don't you search my desk?"

Jack said, "If that's what you'd like me to do. Come with me, please."

Jack led the way to Charlie's desk and opened the top drawer. He pulled out Charlie's Bible, fanning the pages quickly. Several large bills fluttered out of it. Charlie's eyes widened. "That—But—that isn't mine." His voice cracked.

Sean said with a smirk, "He hides behind his religious act, trying to make everyone think he's so holy."

"I have no choice but to terminate you," was all Jack said.

"I don't know why this happened to me, God," he prayed aloud. "This is so unfair. Please help me."

Reflect on this...

What were your thoughts and feelings as you read each story?

Have you ever experienced a time of suffering, sorrow, or pain? If so, how did you deal with the experience?

We pray for our loved ones to be healed. If God chooses not to heal them, how might this affect our faith if at all?

What do you do to encourage others who are suffering? If you are suffering, what would you like others to say or do to encourage you?

Persecution comes in many forms, from discrimination and exclusion to martyrdom. How would you respond if you were Charlie?
Read John 15:18 and 1 Peter 3:14-17.

5

Body of Christ

*But you will receive power
when the Holy Spirit comes on
you; and you will be my witnesses
in Jerusalem, and in all Judea and
Samaria, and to the ends
of the earth.*
Acts 1:8

I was enjoying my evening alone until Steele showed up. I didn't get up off my lawn chair to greet him. I just kept staring out into the darkness. Maybe if I ignored him, he would go away. The guy looked like he was ready to turn tail and run off, like some kids put him up to a game of chicken. I took a sip of my iced tea and winced.

Steele cleared his throat and said, "Hey, Jim." He waved awkwardly with one hand. His other hand was wrapped around the handle of a basket. "Might as well get this over with." I slowly pulled my feet off the porch railing and stood up, dropping my cigar into my glass of sweet tea. Joanne always hated it when I did that, but I hated sweet tea. I only drank it because she said I should try tea instead of what I normally drank.

"Hi," I said back.

"Uh, my wife—she wanted—I mean, she made you something. Thought you might like dinner." He shifted the basket to his other hand.

"Hmm," I answered. I was definitely hungry. Ever since Joanne died, I just didn't feel like making food anymore. I cooked for her the whole time she was sick. Now I lived on frozen dinners and nachos from the bar and grill downtown. I stood up and went to the screen door, reaching in and flipping on the porch light. As long as the guy didn't try to shove his church stuff down my throat, I thought I'd give him a chance.

Steele nodded and took the dish towel off the basket, showing a couple of square glass baking pans. "This one is chicken pot pie, and this is brownies. You like chocolate, right?"

"Yeah," I answered. Joanne must have told them I liked chocolate.

"Well, better go. Have a good night. And I'm sorry about Joanne."

I nodded again. Steele set down the basket by the door and pulled his keys out of his pocket.

That went easier than I thought. I had half expected to hear him say, "I know your wife is gone, but can you still send in her offering checks?" Church was Joanne's thing, not mine. No sir, I had enough of that place years ago. Churches were full of hypocrites, saying one thing on Sunday in their fancy clothes, and then doing exactly what they said they hated every other day of the week.

Sometimes folks from Joanne's church showed up at the door to invite me to picnics and services, but I rarely went because I didn't want anything to do with that. Just five years before Joanne started going there, the minister had left under a dark cloud. News like that gets around fast in a small town. Joanne was a good Christian woman. I couldn't say anything bad about her. But that church bunch. . . I didn't trust them any further than I could throw them. I believe there is a God. It's the rest of the people that are the problem.

People showed up at my door at six o'clock every evening with food for a good two weeks, just like they did the few weeks before Joanne died. Joanne was always doing that for church folks, so I knew what it was about. Someone gets sick or dies, and everyone does the only thing they can think of to do-- they feed them. Not that I minded casserole or pie. I got tired of answering the door, though, and Steele kept coming back. Sometimes he'd bring food, and sometimes he'd ask if I wanted to watch the game with him. I didn't know why. It wasn't like I had done him any favors.

One night Steele showed up early. Too bad I'd planned to walk down to the market. I muttered under my breath and thought about just not answering the door, but the porch light was already on. He had a pizza in one hand and a two-liter bottle of soda in the other.

"Hey. Again," he said. I think he tried to smile, but he looked more like he was afraid I would whack him over the head. He cleared his throat and said, "You like pepperoni?"

"Yeah," I said. "But I was heading down to Grey's Market to get some tomatoes."

"You driving?" he asked.

"No. It's a block away. Why waste gas?"

"Yeah," he said. "Well, the pizza will keep. I'll walk you there. If you want."

"Do what you want."

Steele pulled himself up tall and reached for the screen door, "I'll just stick this in the fridge."

I let him in so he could put the pizza away, and then he followed me out the door.

"Why are you doing this?" I asked.

"Doing what?"

"Following me around like a lost puppy."

"I'm not. But your wife was really important to me. To a lot of people. So you're sorta part of the family."

"I don't want nothin' to do with that church. I told Joanne that, and I bet I told you that, too. Too many hypocrites for my liking."

"Okay. But I still care, ya know. We all do. We miss her."

I bit my tongue a little until the emotions went back down. "Yeah. Well."

"I wish there was something I could do. To help out, I mean."

"Like leaving me alone?"

Steele pretended he didn't hear that one. We arrived at Grey's Market and started toward the fresh food section.

"Matt!" a man yelled from short distance away. "Long time no see!"

"Hey, Bill. How's it goin'?" Steele replied.

"You know that guy?" I said. "I know him from Milligan's bar. How do you know him?"

"Same place," Steele said with a downcast tone in his voice.

"See? Good little church boy on Sunday, barstool warmer on Saturday."

"It's been a long time," Steele said.

"Oh, changing your ways like a good little boy?"

Steele tilted his head. "Well, A.A. You know, 'Hello, my name is Matt, and I'm an alcoholic.' It has been three years since my last drink."

After a pause, he continued, "I'm not proud of my past," he said. "I used to come home drunk and throw things and yell at Missy—that's my wife. So, um, I met Joanne at work—I was a checker at the grocery store. She invited me to church every single time she saw me—for years."

"Yeah, she does...uh...did that."

"Every Sunday morning and night, she asked me, 'You wanna come with?' Course, I always said no. Instead she took notes on the sermon for me and brought me her Sunday school books. I read them sometimes."

"Anyway," Steele continued, "I finally gave in and went. Took the kids to vacation Bible school. It was the persistency of your wife that helped save my life...and my marriage."

"Saved your life?"

"Yeah. There's an addiction recovery group at church. They encouraged me to get help, and they stuck with me through the whole thing."

"I thought everyone was so perfect at church. Except for that pastor who messed up."

"I heard about that. It was way before my time," Steele said. "It's a shame."

"Got that right." I said. "Makes me glad I don't go there. Everyone acts all perfect, but you know they're not."

Steele said, "Look, I don't think you get what church really is. It's one big group of people who discovered God's forgiveness. You know, forgiven sinners helping each other."

"Some more than others," I said with a smirk.

"We are not perfect. However, the church is made up of people who have been forgiven and living every day in obedience to God."[5]

"So once you get forgiven, why bother going back? I'm fine."

---

5. See Acts 2:42-47.

BEAUTY AND THE BROKEN

"People need each other, man. We're not made to be alone. We help each other. And teach each other. And we do our best to follow God together. You should come sometime."

"No thanks. I'm good."

Steele didn't push the issue that night. We made our way through the checkout and walked back to my house, where he got in the car and left. But then he showed up in the morning two days later with fishing poles.

"You fish?" he asked when I came to the screen door.

I sighed and said, "Yeah. I do. Let me get my boots."

It really wasn't so bad, fishing with Steele. He talked, but not too much. As he drove me back home at the end of the day, I asked, "If I go to church with you, will you leave me alone?"

Steele smiled. "Maybe. Uh, probably not. Well, no. I don't think so."

Reflect on this...

What are some of the reasons you have heard people give for staying away from the church? Have you ever used such reasons?

Read Hebrews 10:23-25. How has the body of Christ helped you in your faith journey?

Read 1 Corinthians 12:12-27. When a body moves, all its parts are needed and move together. How might this change the way people think of church?

What do you feel is your role in the body of Christ?

If you have ever lived apart from the body of Christ, how does this differ from life as a part of the body?

6

Social Holiness

Each of you should give what you have decided in your heart to give, not reluctantly or under compulsion, for God loves a cheerful giver.
2 Corinthians 9:7

Max found the city fascinating. It was complex and full of contrasts--rich and poor, young and old, artists and business people, danger and goodwill. Flawed as it was, it had been his home for the past two years. While he missed his parents and sister, he did not miss the cold Wisconsin winter--not when January in southern California was this warm. He enjoyed walking the mile from his new apartment to his job in the office at the museum. As he made his way down the palm tree lined street, he passed unique shops, musicians, cafes, and beggars with their often inventive slogans on cardboard signs.

At lunch time, Max frequented a nearby restaurant that the tourists usually overlooked. It was a dive, but it had excellent, cheap food. He seriously doubted he would find a better--or bigger--burrito anywhere in the metro area. And he had a thing for cinnamon coffee, which was abundant there. The servers even poured some of it into a to-go cup for him most days. Then Max would carry half his lunch and coffee back to work. Dinner usually consisted of lunch leftovers, which was just fine with Max. A chef he was not, and he had school loans to repay.

On one day in particular, as Max left the restaurant, he saw a man in a green army jacket sitting on the sidewalk. He seemed to be sleeping propped up against the front of the restaurant with his hoodie pulled up over his eyes. He was also holding onto the leash of a big, yellow dog in one bony, filthy hand. The hastily scrawled cardboard sign next to him read, "Bet you can't hit me with a quarter!"

Max normally tried not to look at the beggars. He felt torn between knowing God would want him to help and not knowing if the money he gave would go toward drugs or booze. But he smiled at this guy's sign. He dropped a few coins into the cup next to it and went on his way, wondering why the man was begging so far out of the way when there was better money to be made on the more heavily-traveled blocks. Beggars usually sat near the high-end businesses where people had more cash to shell out and might be a little more generous.

The way Max looked at it, begging was as much a business as anything else. He was sure that half these guys, especially ones with funny signs, were pros. They probably had apartments of their own. Maybe they didn't want to find jobs because they made better money begging. He had heard about a saxophone player in Chicago who made enough money playing on the street to save up and buy a condo on the lake front.

Max dug through his pocket for some change and dropped it into the cup in front of the cardboard sign. The dog sniffed at his box of leftovers and licked its chops as Max bent down to give his money. For a second, he thought of handing it over, but the thought of the poor dog after eating beans and hot sauce was enough to stop him.

"Thanks, man," the guy said as he turned to leave.

"Uh, yeah. Don't worry about it," Max said. There was something about that voice. Max wanted to go back and see who the man was, but he had a meeting in fifteen minutes. He hurried on his way.

The next day, Max saw the same guy sitting outside the restaurant. The words "anything helps" were added in smaller letters at the bottom of the sign. He began to feel guilty. Didn't this guy know he'd get more change up the street? Unsure what to do with himself; he answered a few texts as he passed and entered the building. When he left, he did the same thing as the day before, dropping the sixty cents' change he got inside the restaurant into the beggar's cup.

"God bless you," the guy said without looking up. The man had on a baseball cap under his hoodie this time, and he never looked up.

Max felt his face flush immediately. God blessed him, that was sure. Couldn't he do better for this guy who didn't seem to have a clue how to beg? There were very few coins in the cup. He cleared his throat and held out his leftover box. "Hey, man. You want this?"

The beggar didn't look up at him. He just said, "Naw, man. I'm good."

Max awkwardly pulled back his lunch and with an "Uh, okay," walked away. Halfway down the block, Max stopped, eyes wide. He knew that voice. He was sure of it. He doubled back to where the beggar sat.

The beggar didn't look up when he stopped in front of him, so Max bent down a little, trying to get a good look at him.

"I know you, don't I?"

With that, the beggar looked up, and Max exclaimed, "Sam!"

"'Sup," he said simply with a nod. Sam's face was thinner than it should have been and hidden behind an unruly red beard, but that was definitely the Sam who had been his first roommate at college. His eyes looked different somehow. Older, maybe, as though he had seen rough times.

"How'd you get here? I mean, where have you been? I never saw you again after freshman year."

"You know I flunked out," he said.

"I guess," Max answered. "Have you been here all this time?"

"Naw. I tried the Army."

"Really?" Then Max sputtered, "I'm sorry. It's just-- Well, you didn't seem the type to be into that."

"I know, right? Waking up early, PT before dawn? But it was pretty cool, actually. Well, after basic training. But then I blew out my knee in infantry school." The dog shifted in its sleep, and Sam reached over and rubbed its side.

"Whoa."

"Yeah," Sam agreed, nodding. "After that, nothing worked out. Can't work much with my knee like this, and can't get it fixed. I figured if I gotta be on the streets, I might as well thumb a ride to a warmer place."

"Huh." Max thought for a minute. "Wait. What about your parents? Can't you go to them?"

Sam scoffed, and Max didn't push him any further. "So where are you staying?"

"Don't worry about it. I'm alright."

"You sure?"

"Yeah. But thanks, man."

"Hey, I need to--" I gestured up the street with my thumb.

"Yeah, go on. See you around, man. Thanks for stopping."

"Yeah. Good to see you."

Max made it through the afternoon at work on autopilot, not quite focusing on what he was doing. Even if Max hadn't seen Sam in years, he was still a friend. Max couldn't just have his buddy begging, could he? He tossed and turned in his bed. He wanted to invite Sam to stay with him, but was he trustworthy now?

"What do I do God?" Max prayed aloud.

Sam had been his roommate at college, and he had introduced him to all his friends. When they had gone camping that early spring and one of the guys lost his backpack to a flooded stream, Sam had shared his extra dry clothes and gear. Now Sam was in a place where he had lost everything. Max fell asleep knowing what he was going to do.

The next day, Max took the afternoon off work and went back to the restaurant. He got two huge burritos and two cinnamon coffees to go. Balancing all of this, he backed out the door and walked up to Sam. He set the food and drinks on the ground and sat down next to his friend.

"You still like burritos, right?" Max asked.

"You know it. Thanks, man," Sam started in on his burrito eagerly, pulling a few pieces of meat out for his dog.

The two ate in silence for a while, ignoring the varied looks they got from people who passed them.

Finally, Max took a long swig of coffee and said, "So I have an apartment with an extra bedroom. Why don't you stay at my place for a little while until we can get you back on your feet?"

Reflect on this...

How do you respond to beggars or the homeless on the street? Do you try to help them? Do you turn away and avoid making eye contact? Why do you think you react the way you do?

In this story, Max refused to get involved with beggars until the beggar was someone he knew. In what ways do even the most well-meaning Christians fail to see the poor as individual people?

Read Matthew 25:31-40. What we do for the needy, Jesus says we are doing for Him. How might awareness of this affect how we deal with the less fortunate?

What keeps people from helping the needy?

Read Proverbs 14:31 and 19:17. Not everyone has money to give to the poor, but giving money is not the only way to help. What else can you do to be kind to the needy?

NOTES:

7

Overcoming Your Past

Therefore, if anyone is in Christ,
the new creation has come: The
old has gone, the new is here!
2 Corinthians 5:17

"This is a job. Just a job," I told myself aloud, white-knuckling the steering wheel as I sat in the parking lot of the Country Club. My ten-year high school reunion. It would have been so easy to leave if not for the money I was getting to take pictures. Any income was better than none. Running a small business was not easy.

"Jesus, be my strength," I whispered as I got out of the car and made my big entrance to the reunion, so loaded down with equipment, I felt like a pack mule. The tripod and photography umbrella kept threatening to slip out from under my arms. Someone, a man, saw me coming and held the door open.

"Thanks," I said quietly as I passed.

"Wait. Amy?" The guy called after me incredulously, and I stopped. My stomach felt heavy and knotted up.

I took a deep breath through my nose and smiled widely. "That's me," I replied, turning. He looked familiar, but I wasn't sure of his name.

"Chad," the guy said, pointing at the name tag on his shirt. "Remember? Tailgating at the homecoming game and the prom after-party? That one party where someone called the cops and the cops called your parents?"

I winced a little and tried to tuck the photography umbrella further up under my arm. I succeeded only in dropping everything that wasn't strapped onto me. Chad quickly bent down to pick everything up.

"I got it, I got. Why don't I help you help you carry this?" he offered.

"Um, sure. Thanks," I said.

"You know, I didn't expect to see you. . . you know, here," Chad said.

The bottom dropped out of my stomach. "Yeah?" I asked, clearing my throat.

"I mean, I figured you'd end up—I don't know. . ."

"Dead by 21?"

"Or something. Jail, maybe," he added with a chuckle.

"Well, I'm not. Thankfully. I'll take that from here." I set down my bag and reached for the rest of my equipment.

"A photographer. . . Who knew?"

I sighed. "Who knew," I answered.

As much as I tried to leave all the stupid stuff I did in the past, everyone in Southern Hills was determined to remind me of it. I was so glad I didn't live here anymore. If I'd had ten dollars for every time someone said, "Amy? You're still alive?" or "Wow, I didn't expect to see you again" or "Remember that one party you threw? It was epic!" that night, I would have been able to quit my photography business and live off that.

As I stopped by tables and photographed groups of my former classmates, I found myself more and more glad that I had my camera to hide behind. Some people stopped talking altogether when I came near, and several of the women looked me over from head to toe as they said smiling pleasantries and went back to their conversations. They didn't remember my name; they only remembered not trusting me around their boyfriends. My camera was the only thing that made me feel less exposed. People forget the photographer in their excitement to pose for the camera.

After a while, Chad came back to me with someone I recognized all too well—Tony. I had gotten into my fair share of trouble with Tony, doing all sorts of things for which I had been forgiven by God and would never do again. But Tony had no way of knowing that at first sight. He moved his head to the side and smiled as I quickly shook his hand and went back to hiding behind my camera.

"Amy," Tony said, catching me lightly by the sleeve. "A bunch of us are getting together upstairs later tonight. You know, play some cards, have some drinks. You game?"

"I don't think so" I said politely as I inwardly screamed, NO!

"What, don't you want to reminisce with us? Old times. Weren't' they great?"

I shook my head in such a way as to indicate feelings of disagreement with his statement.

"What, don't you party?" Tony asked.

"Not anymore," I said awkwardly.

Tony's eyebrows shot up, and D'Shon stepped into the group with Tamara on his arm. I hadn't expected those two to end up together! Tamara was the quiet, bookworm type and never ran in the circles that D'Shon—or I—did. Though I was never actually a part of the circle. I just made them laugh and partied with them on occasion. Aside from that, I doubted any of them knew anything about me.

"Milano," the guy said. They did this weird handshake, half-hug thing and bumped chests.

"S.H. High Pythons, Sssssssss!" they both called. A few hoots and whistles rose up around the banquet hall. I tried not to roll my eyes. What were we, teenagers?

D'Shon finally noticed me and said, "Amy! You comin' up later?"

"She says she doesn't party," Tony said a little too loudly over the nostalgic playlist I was pretty sure had been played at every dance during high school. "Don't worry, girl, I got your back," he said with a conspiratorial wink and a pat on my back. I stepped away from his hand.

"Well that's a surprise," Shelby something-or-other said, joining the group that was starting to cluster around me. Sweat broke out on my forehead and back. "When would this ridiculous reunion be over so I could go home?"

"What, did she find Jesus?" someone muttered. D'Shon and Tony laughed, and Tamara just looked down at her feet uncomfortably.

"Naw, we'll get her to change her mind," Tony said, patting me on the back again. "A tiger can't change its stripes!"

"Crush the Tigers," someone yelled to another chorus of "Woo!"

"Amy! I've been looking for you! Can you come get a picture?" another woman's voice said. I felt myself being pulled by the arm, back and away from the group. I whirled around, ready to give a piece of my mind to the next person who gave even a little grief. I stopped short when I saw that I was standing face to face with Vicky.

I felt awful about most of the things I'd done in high school, but not nearly as awful as I felt about what I had done to Vicky. Vicky, the good girl whose locker was next to mine. I had called her all kinds of names. Vicky was a part of the study hall prayer group and the debate team. I had teased her relentlessly whenever our paths had crossed, even though she had never done anything to me. Vicky had never even stood up to me.

"I'm glad to see you," she said without a look at the others. With her arm still linked through mine, she led me across the room to a table in the far corner, near where my equipment was set up for group portraits, which I would begin taking later.

She dropped her purse onto the table and said to a tall man who had left another group to join her, "Amy, this is my husband, Dan. And Dan, this is Amy. She goes to Fellowship Church." Then, to me, "Didn't I see you doing face painting at Hope Fest?"

I blinked a few times. "Um, yeah. I do. And I was there. But I didn't see you." My shoulders loosened up a little at the mention of my new life.

"Oh, we ran the rock climbing wall," Vicky said. "There wasn't much time to visit that day."

Dan excused himself as someone called him over. When he was gone, I asked Vicky, "Why are you doing this?"

"Doing what?" Vicky asked.

"Being nice to me. I was so horrible to you all through school."

Vicky thought for a moment and said, "Well, because that was the past. You're a believer now, aren't you?"

I nodded. "I am so sorry for the way I treated you."

"I forgave you long ago. And God forgives you. All the stuff you did back then, that isn't you anymore. You're a new creation. I heard what those guys were saying back there, and it is a lie. People can change. God can change anyone. Even them." Vicky nodded toward the group we'd left. When I looked up, Tony nodded at me and raised a glass into the air.

I met her eyes, and she smiled at me. I returned her smile. "Thanks. I appreciate that."

Sometime later, Tony, Chad, D'Shon, and a few others came over for a group portrait. I squared my shoulders as I stood and led them to the photo area I had set up in the corner. Vicky reached out as I passed her and gave my hand a quick squeeze. "I'm a new creation, I thought."

"Party starts in an hour. You coming up?" Tony asked.

I smiled and replied, "No, thanks."

Reflect on this...

Have you ever felt like Amy? If so, how did you work through those thoughts and feelings?

Read 2 Corinthians 5:17. How does the idea of becoming a "new creation" differ from the world's idea of overcoming the past?

What are some of the things that make people believe they cannot leave a sinful past behind? How can others have an influence on how we deal with our past?

Read Acts 9:17-22, 26-27. Saul was a dramatically new person after his conversion, but some people struggled to accept his change. Share a story of someone who has been radically saved and changed by Jesus.

What, if anything, holds you back from accepting that you are a new creation in Christ?

NOTES:

The DIALOG SERIES

offers topical and biblical small group studies that generate meaningful conversation. Each 7–week study explores a subject significant to the church and to the story of God. Dialog *creates community. So let's talk.*

SEVEN DEADLY SINS

This study looks closely at seven of the most common sins people struggle with, and explores ways in which we can avoid, deal with, and overcome each one through the power of God.

- - - - - - - - - -

Participant's Guide 978-0-8341-3538-3
Facilitator's Guide   978-0-8341-3537-6

BEAUTY AND THE BROKEN

Beauty and the Broken tells 7 true-to-life stories of ordinary people. Each narrative is designed to help you ponder the deep questions our struggles raise, and find hope and beauty in your own experiences.

- - - - - - - - - -

Participant's Guide 978-0-8341-3430-0
Facilitator's Guide   978-0-8341-3429-4

PRESSURE POINTS

Pressure Points digs deep into the areas of life that have a profound impact on us and examines practical ways we can face each challenge successfully.

- - - - - - - - - -

Participant's Guide 978-0-8341-3536-9
Facilitator's Guide   978-0-8341-3535-2

HOLY LIVING

This study examines what it truly means to live a Christlike life. Holiness is more about surrender than being perfect—it's about obedience rather than religious performance.

- - - - - - - - - -

Participant's Guide 978-0-8341-3432-4
Facilitator's Guide   978-0-8341-3431-7

OTHER TITLES AVAILABLE

THE BEATITUDES
Participant's Guide 978-0-8341-3374-7
Facilitator's Guide   978-0-8341-3373-0

CHRISTIAN DISCIPLINES
Participant's Guide 978-0-8341-2980-1
Facilitator's Guide   978-0-8341-2986-3

ELEPHANTS IN THE CHURCH
Participant's Guide 978-0-8341-2979-5
Facilitator's Guide   978-0-8341-2985-6

TAKE UP YOUR MAT
Participant's Guide 978-0-8341-2981-8
Facilitator's Guide   978-0-8341-2987-0

THE STORY OF GOD
Participant's Guide 978-0-8341-3351-8
Facilitator's Guide   978-0-8341-3350-1

FAITH AMONG FRIENDS
Participant's Guide 978-0-8341-3139-2
Facilitator's Guide   978-0-8341-3140-8

SEARCHING FOR ANSWERS
Participant's Guide 978-0-8341-3372-3
Facilitator's Guide   978-0-8341-3371-6

THE PROPHETS
Participant's Guide 978-0-8341-3376-1
Facilitator's Guide   978-0-8341-3375-4

SUIT UP
Participant's Guide 978-0-8341-3141-5
Facilitator's Guide   978-0-8341-3142-2

THE SOWER WENT OUT
Participant's Guide 978-0-8341-3102-6
Facilitator's Guide   978-0-8341-3101-9

REVELATION
Participant's Guide 978-0-8341-3143-9
Facilitator's Guide   978-0-8341-3144-6

THE FRUIT OF THE SPIRIT
Participant's Guide 978-0-8341-3100-2
Facilitator's Guide   978-0-8341-3099-9

EVERYDAY CHRISTIAN
Participant's Guide 978-0-8341-3098-2
Facilitator's Guide   978-0-8341-3097-5

Order online at DialogSeries.com or by phone at 1-800-877-0700.